A CIRCLE OF SISTAZ

The Evolution of a Poet
Vol. 1

Yvonne Jackson (Allen)

A Circle of Sistaz
The Evolution of a Poet
Vol. 1

Copyright © 2012 by Yvonne Ranee Jackson
Published by Bennu Rising Publishing
Printed by CreateSpace, an Amazon Co.

Bennu Rising Publishing
P.O. Box 35125
Detroit, Michigan 48235

Copyright © 2012 by Yvonne Ranee Jackson
Rights & Permissions Bennu Rising Publishing

All rights reserved. This book and any portion thereof may not be reproduced without written permission of the owner. Contact Bennu Rising Publishing for more information.

This book contains performance material. Any unauthorized use of the title, copyrighted material, and its content without written permission is prohibited.

Cover Design by Melissa Talbot
Edited by Gloria Palmer
Printed by CreateSpace, an Amazon.com Company
Available from Amazon.com

Manufactured in the United States of America

For more information about books from Bennu Rising Publishing email: Bennupub@yahoo.com

ISBN-13: 978-0-9916646-0-3

DEDICATION

Adrienne, Triva, Travia, Aronda, Monique, Patricia, Kim

CONTENTS

- ♥ Acknowledgments — vii
- ♥ Preface — ix

The Lovers

- ♥ Art Work — 1
- ♥ Ricochet — 2
- ♥ Curious — 3
- ♥ Mental Climax — 4
- ♥ First Love — 5
- ♥ Full Circle — 6
- ♥ In My Dreams — 7
- ♥ The Attraction — 8
- ♥ Husband — 9
- ♥ Finally — 10

The Strugglers

- ♥ The Mirror — 13
- ♥ Broken — 14
- ♥ Leaving — 15
- ♥ Misery — 16
- ♥ Ghetto Life, Hood Strife — 17
- ♥ Infidelity — 18
- ♥ The Underground — 19

The Overcomers

- ♥ Rivalry — 23
- ♥ Bag Lady — 24
- ♥ What I Want — 25
- ♥ A Letter to My Father — 26

- ♥ About the Author — 27

ACKNOWLEDGMENTS

I'd like to give thanks to God first for giving me the ability to take experiences and put them on paper. What a blessing it is. I would like to acknowledge all the wonderful people who had something to do with making this literary art piece possible for me. I couldn't have made it without any of you. It makes me happy to know you all cared about a dream of mine.

To my children, thank you all for putting up with all the screaming, hollering, and frustration. Nene, keep singing and living the dream. Know that it is never too late. Lele, you have given me strength through this process. Janai, Tavis, and Travia, Mommy loves you. Most of all thanks for putting up with all the sistaz in me.

To my biggest influence for this book, Johnny, thanks for giving me the experiences. Ironic, I know, but poetic justice to say the least. I thank God for carrying me through.

To Mommy, I love you more than words can express. To all my sisters, my stories and poetry are inspired by who we are and the things we experience. I remember and give thanks to you.

To Billy, it started with you. Thanks for giving me your touch. The man behind the healing. To my soulmate, Joseph, I love you and you have shown me how I should be loved. I thank God for second chances.

To Tish, for crying those tears with me and listening to so many of my stories. My son, Keem, for giving me your ear and for hearing beyond the words. Buddy, for listening day in and day out. You are a good listener. To all my friends and family who supported me in making this book a reality.

To Tonja, you have inspired me through the projects and work you do. I can't thank you enough. Melissa, you are the bomb. Thanks for your professional design expertise and willingness. To Gloria. I am so glad you are a part of this literary work. Richard, you are the wizard of projects and I thank you for just being you.

Finally, thanks to my publisher, Bennu Rising Publishing, for being my first. Bigger things are coming.

PREFACE

Initially, this project started out as individual poetry pieces, never intended to be put together as a book. I wrote to relieve stress and each piece was placed for a long time in a folder. The idea for the book *A Circle of Sistaz* came about in 2010. What started as a coping mechanism became a story told in a way that gave birth to artistry in words.

In 2004, devastation hit and my pen started working again for the first time since my college years during the late 80's, early 90's. It turned out to be one of the best ideas for me. I put this first volume of poetry and spoken word together with the hopes of influencing someone in a positive way through different emotions and stories. It will give the reader a peek into the trials many of us go through in life and some of the good times as well. There is something here for everyone who reads it.

A Circle of Sistaz is definitely for the "keep-it-real people". This book contains real issues. An open mind and heart will help it accomplish its goal. Not a book for kids though. There are pieces in this book that I wrote early on, and we all know the different levels of life we face at some time or another. No one is perfect, right?

The idea was a long time coming. It was a struggle for years to even get the idea in action. Part of the hesitation was making sure the reader got it, that people understood *A Circle of Sistaz* exists in many of us. The most important thing is to embrace all the parts of our personality, learning from them, and ultimately growing from it as a whole. In 2012, I threw all caution to the wind and put my mind, hands, and determination together, and this book *A Circle of Sistaz* was born.

A CIRCLE OF SISTAZ

THE LOVERS

ART WORK

You caught my eye before words were spoken. It was the essence of your soul that I had chosen to be a part of in this way. Like a drug addict living life on the street day to day.

I fear this will soon end and I won't pretend I don't love you because I do. With every deep seed in my soul, you make me whole.

I have no life without you in it, and when we touch, I'm rendered speechless. To run away is pointless because my feet won't move, especially when you're in my groove, touching me, feeling me, spoiling me with your tongue. I have become sprung on the thoughts of you.

You work me like a charm in arms that I lose control over what this is all about. Your intellect has me turned out.

Hands that move up my thighs, teasing the diamond that sits on top. I pop the question of you and me. Can this work? Will there ever be a time when you're never on my mind?

And when you leave can I go back to the way things were without thinking how it might have been? You're no doubt my friend, but what if I were to say that with you I want to stay?

Could you handle that? Would your structured life remain intact? Who can put constraints on how I feel when my heart you steal? With all these elements to consider, leaving me anyway, would it make me bitter?

What we have created, never unstated, are pieces of art, so don't tell me you don't feel it just as I; your defenses I won't buy.

I feel it in your kiss and the way you touch me, so can we really play it smart and throw away this priceless piece of art?

RICOCHET

Running down the halls of my mind, I stumble on the fact that I have fallen for you and you aren't mine.
I know I laid down the rules that over time have made me the fool.
No commitment is the shit I spit but not the way I feel.
    I want a man who makes me feel real.
I have been honest with you but not with myself, and with each day I die because of it.
I was willing to share you, care for you, and now I dare you to leave her for me, can't you see?
I have become your destiny.
    I have become your lover, your friend, yours again.
    I know I said no labels but that is what we are.
    Like a student earning a degree.
You have graduated and I hate it because, deep down inside, you won't choose me.
    I have redefined a buddy.
I recite spoken-word poetry to you all the time, but this one you will never hear because I can't and won't let you know what's on my mind.
So I'll take what you give and hope that with just that I can live—occasional weekend stays, while your real girl is away.
Making love under the covers, and damn, you are such a good lover.
I want more than to be a closet hoe and I think just in the small amount of time you know.
Why did you have to touch me like that, lick me like that, feel me like that?
Now I'm stuck in this trap. I thought I had you, but you got me. I'm the result of a lover's ricochet.

CURIOUS

From the moment you passed, I wanted to know you.
    The attraction was so true.
I've masturbated to the very thought
    of your touch between my thighs, flowing on magical highs
I have fantasized you going deep into my halls of fame with
    only one name
That name is ecstasy; your presence gets the best of me and
    I don't mind, but in reality
    you are just a friend to me
    I don't want to break that bond
As you speak, I watch your lips move
    and it is like a magician with his wand
    controlling everything
You make my words twist as I speak and even choke
    Damn! I think I want to deep throat
You are so real and you are the type of man I can deal
    but you are spoken for and so am I
    It would complicate things, we can't deny
I get wet because the love has got to be good
    you're an intellectual with just a touch of hood
They say curiosity killed the cat and I wouldn't mind you
    doing exactly that
Beating it up, down, and all around
    Oooh, do you realize how good that shit sounds?
This is mysterious, the temptation serious,
    and me I'm simply curious

Yvonne Jackson (Allen)

MENTAL CLIMAX

Here I am thinking of you and how many times I've fucked you—no, excuse me, made love to you—in my mind.

Every time I think of you my hips swerve and my lips curl between the clamps of my teeth and I can't seem to stop myself.

It's been years of what ifs and how it might have beens, now all I can concentrate on is you and the way you grab my . . . mmmmm!

Oh how I miss that shit and all that is you, touching a side of me that is and will always be, in my pusssss—sorry can't say that, won't say that.

It has taken me years and a bottle of Remy to get to this point, and I don't even know if you are taking this to heart.

Like I said, he is not you; I love you and only you can make me feel this way. If I could erase my life with him up to this point, I would replace it with you and your lean, mean poking machine.

You don't have a clue what it is you do to me when you speak the words of tranquility. Don't be afraid to touch me like you use to because I am your playground.

I can't see someone else loving you, touching you, even though it turns me on to know that someone else is failing at what I mastered years ago. Far away in the depths of my soul, you were the one who let me do what I wanted to do.

Ohhhhh! I think I want to cum at the very thought of your clever temptation towards me. Don't think of me as his girl but think of me as your woman in the midst of my climax, your climax, our cum.

FIRST LOVE

I remember you, love, like the memory of a distant star that
    shines in the sky.
I lost my breath for just a moment when you caught my
    eye.
It was like the freshness in the air after it rains
    and I could see you in my arms again.
We made love over and over.
    I lived life like a drunk trying to stay sober.
Except I was addicted to your muscular back
    and ooh, baby, the instrument you pack.
You see to me you were a musician who played the keys
    on my mmm . . . and I sang the melody loud;
    you took me bouncing in the air from cloud to cloud.
I wish I could put it into words the way you made
    me feel; yeah, daddy, it was so unreal.
Don't get me wrong, it wasn't just a physical thang.
    No, it was one of those loves that made my heart sang.
Your words flowed from your head and I listen as you
    read.
You read the thoughts and I absorbed them, taking me to
    a whole different level.
I let go with you and all that you were
    but I never saw in our future a break up would
    occur.
In one instant you were gone. No more would we play
    that song.
I sit here fifteen years later thinking of you. Even though
    it was to another I said I do, I don't have one regret.
The love I had with you I will never forget. I know I can
    no long fly high on your embrace high above. I just
    had to let you know you are my first love.

Yvonne Jackson (Allen)

FULL CIRCLE

I didn't realize how much I loved you until now, it is years later, and to another man I have given my vow

To love, honor, and cherish forever, and I did because I thought our future would be never

Again I am faced with this critical moment of truth—whether it be to myself, him, or you

We gave up love years into our past, don't remember the date or specific time I saw you last

But I remember the moments we spent and how surreal it was when with another your love went

It left me sad with an empty hole in my heart; I owed it to myself to get a new start

You were the first I ever loved; lying in my bed at night, I cried often to the moon above

Hoping that somehow the memory of you would soon let me go; it only grew deeper, and in my mind, your face I sowed

I moved on and fell in love again, experienced happiness and the pain

I never could have imagined the day I would see you once more, how would it feel when you walked through that door

And on occasion we speak, avoiding the consequences of the things that would happen if we meet

So I still wait for something that I thirst and will my now-love give me up first

I'll wait for that lifelong miracle; I'll wait for our lives to come full circle

IN MY DREAMS

In my dreams you are all I'll ever want and need
In my dreams I feel you in me, with me, teasing me
In my dreams you deliver it all with one breath
In my dreams I taste the very essence that had me sprung
In my dreams you watch me with intensity
In my dreams I gesture for your response
In my dreams you give me only a kiss here and a kiss there
In my dreams I am your friend and you are mine
In my dreams you have had other lovers' sweet and kind
In my dreams I fantasize of encounters that may never be
In my dreams we will stay for eternity

Yvonne Jackson (Allen)

THE ATTRACTION

To watch you walk is heaven with a twist of paradise, and
 when you enter the room, I get a sense of butterflies.
I seek a comfort zone hoping you don't notice, that in
 your presence, I am hopeless.
Hopelessly looking for an acknowledgement, what is this
 attraction? With you, I am spent.
I pause for a moment to take into account that my hair is
 just right and lipstick the perfect amount.
I have always been that woman in control but not
 any more; it is you I want to explore.
I want to touch you, hold you, hmmm . . .
 believe me when I say what I would do to you in
 harmony; yeah, it's got the best of me.
This isn't just a physical thang, so much more than that;
 it takes you to make me purr like a cat.
I have to keep my dignity in place, no emotions worn on
 my face.
A million ways to let you know how I feel; then a span of
 silence from you, I had to deal.
Now at this moment I'll throw caution to the wind
 and pray a response you will send.
I'm using my talent to get the message through,
 that I think the world of you.

HUSBAND

When we first met, it was on my mind that in time I would capture you with just a look. The joke was on me because you took my breath away. I prayed you would stay and the idea you would leave I couldn't conceive. My day-to-day existence relied on you and you on me. We came to be good friends and decided to be until life would end. 'Til death do us part you have my heart and I love you more now than ever before. Sure trials come and go, to test and show that we are stronger. Now I understand that God had His hand in this from the start; you are my heart. We have built this life together through all types of weather. Let no man put us under; you are my thunderbolt and fight beside me on every hand…. you are without a doubt a true husband.

Yvonne Jackson (Allen)

FINALLY

You were smooth with your tall, handsome self
You were the card in a good hand that I was dealt
I kept my composure as you held me on the dance floor
Ooooh, the feel of your body I could not ignore

Finally

It was at that moment I fell for you
And it was your mind I wanted to do
We dated briefly and in a moment you moved in
I didn't care at all, living without you the real sin

Finally

Two years later we became one
And I felt the joy of being your one…and only
It wasn't too long before the test for us started
A couple of blows almost had us parted

Finally

But with every break-up a child came
And our love would never be the same
As I sit here nine years later
I know there's no human love greater

Finally

Will we make it? Many aren't sure
But our love has conquered and endured
I love you with all my heart and everything that's in me
Because I've found my soul mate…

FINALLY!

THE STRUGGLERS

THE MIRROR

How do I rid myself of the pain inside? Memories of a happy life locked away and a smile that tears hide.

We live our lives with hopes of successful dreams and drown them in failures' misery streams.

I stand and look through this glass at the bruises and I love you is the excuse he uses.

I loved a man too much and that is now my crime. He has taken my soul; it is no longer mine.

With every blow of his fist, I told myself, it is mind over matter. But it never worked; only my heart would shatter.

Is this love? I had asked myself to be sure. How much more can one endure?

I've prayed and God has turned his back. I've even attempted to leave, my bags I have packed.

But there's no use for me to leave. He'll only find me; a death sentence I'll receive.

So I'll break this mirror reflection I see and the pain can then be relieved of me.

I took a piece of the glass from the floor. It will be over for me soon, horror no more.

I watched my blood run from my wrists. He can't hurt me any more, for this is final bliss.

There's no other way out, no more tears to cry.
My final moment, my freedom is to die.

BROKEN

There are weeds growing long in the yard
no flowers in the tear-stained soil outside the window
The doors are closed and locked
and they protect the loneliness inside
You are a hypnotist; I am lost in time
You controlled my mind

The paint is chipped around the walls
each empty room holds the secrets of a love gone wrong
The dust covers the shelves
where romantic stories once roamed
You are a champion fighter, I took the blows
You battered my body and no one knows

A chill has settled throughout this place
The wind carries the melody of cries inside the attic panes
Nothing but silence travels the halls
and a history of impressionable laughter
You are the devil himself; I was condemned

You stole my soul

Where do I go from here? How do I live?
You left my home; my heart filled with tears . . .
Broken

LEAVING

I look in your eyes and see you have decided to go. It seems to be the only thing you know. Go away, leave me and your three children behind. The funny thing is, if I left, would you mind? It is nothing new to me, you know, that your sorry, unconcerned ass is leaving. You slam the door. The door of opportunity and life. Your actions stab into the bare essence of my soul like a knife. Who the fuck did I think I was to you? I thought I was your wife. Your heart, your lungs, your mind.

At that moment, I realized it would be different this time. Time is on my side now. I take a breath as I brush across my brow. I stand in this hallway this night and look at the back of your heels as they hit the pavement with every step. It's like a jab from Mike, hitting me left then right. It has been twelve years of the same old shit, and like a junkie, I take the hit.

Every time I bare your child you choose to leave me, which would make you leave me times three. Is it the concept of fatherhood that makes you bitch up? To some degree, a responsibility is what you have to live up. But that's okay because you'll come back, and I'll try to keep my dignity intact. I can't go on with you over and over again. The death of our marriage is in your hands. I'll cry my tears until you return, but like the soulful song goes, maybe we should just let it burn.

Yvonne Jackson (Allen)

MISERY

I push these feeling to the center of my mind hoping they won't surface, praying they don't surface

I have offended you and I am sorry, for all that I have cost you, all in which I have cost myself

I knew the consequence of my endless desire to have some part of you in my life

But how can I lose you without losing myself? My true self can only exist with you and no one else

You are who makes me feel comfortable. You make me feel right

I think about you all the time for that is where the truth exists, yet I live each day a lie

Hoping time passes until this ends, no more lies, no more thoughts of you, of me

Does it end, my love, or is it a continuous punishment that I live in? Show me, love, how to put a stop to the thoughts of you and me. Take me out of this sad but truth of a misery.

GHETTO LIFE, HOOD STRIFE

Tat tat tat ta tat are the sounds outside my window, the
    stench of rotten animal corpses when the wind blow
Deep in my heart, I love this life I've come to know
    Why do we stay? How can we go far so emotions
    don't show?
This is the life in the ghetto, the life that we deny,
    another bootleg CD, on Friday night, gettin high
It is what I live fo, die fo, cry fo, lie fo,
    so no one can come here unless they have fear fo
Drugs in my streets, hookers walkin the beat
    but this hell is what I love under my feet
Young boy shot, one to the chest, two to the fo'head
    momma cryin 'cause he's dead
Everybody wants to see the crime-scene tape,
    never realizing the display of hate
These are the things we show each other,
    sister to sister and brother to brother
Sirens every night, Ms. Johnson thinks no one knows
    she's hitting the pipe, knowin using her social security
    ain't all right
My bridge card is now half full, had to sell some of it off,
    bill collectors aren't takin no bull
I have a job to pay my rent; production is down, my sugar
    daddy waitin on his payback for money he spent
I'll play him off for as long as I can; hell, he doesn't even
    know he ain't really my man
Naw he ain't; you see my man is a hustler, pants-hangin,
    draws-showin, blunt-smokin, pussy-eatin struggler
Every now and then, he hits a good lick; he knows I'm
    his big-booty, ride-or-die chick
You know I've never been out of the hood; if I had the
    chance, can't say I would go, cause this is all I know

. . . The life in the ghetto.

Yvonne Jackson (Allen)

INFIDELITY

It's half past nine and I didn't sleep last night;
>the smile on my face says I'm fine but my heart isn't right. I wonder how long I can wait for you, always true, still your ass left me blue.

It's been a year since I've seen your face; you lie and say in
>your heart I have a place. Is it your impression of me? It's getting the best of me, slowly killing me emotionally.

My soul has to grow, my heart yearns to go, but it is
>wounded by your selfish blow. Years of tears I have cried, 'til the wells of my eyes have dried, so I hide the pain you've given me behind thoughts of infidelity.

Like a hound on the trail of a scent, my nose was open
>wide, my head spent. I longed for you in me, one we could be, but that is not how the story ends—you've left me to your best friend. He's always around and it is to his body I'm bound.

I'm finding it's hard to not entertain; in the heat of things
>he softly calls my name. Yes, my love, he is my pacifier; on his down stroke, I am higher than the trees you see; it is he who completes me, and your absence has slowly driven me to infidelity.

THE UNDERGROUND

You tried to damage me
        beat me down with your antics of evolution,
        revolution, polluting the very virgin depths of
        my mind
You spoke, I listened, and with every word,
        you closed the door of my mind, leaving me
        paralyzed and out of control
        I was no longer myself,
        changing into a weak-minded girl
You said with your knowledge I could be free
        Free from me and all the evils of
        the Babylonic theories that imprisoned me
You took my identity and gave me demons
        that scratched and clawed at the very essence
        of my soul
I was looking searching for a spiritual fantasy,
        not the deep hell that encamped me while I
        remained in your bars. Yes, prison that is what
        it was for me
Living on beaches with a washed-up actress
        who the only consistency she had was her lock of
        hair she carried in a bag
You sang songs of Rastafari but knew nothing of
        what God really meant, yet you called yourself a
        prophet
I was afraid of you yet intrigued because the magnitude
        of insanity was uncanny
I realized the names Jim Jones and Koresh were
        that of your name and the same
        I had to get away, get out, soon
        before I died

. . . Spiritually

Yvonne Jackson (Allen)

THE OVERCOMERS

RIVALRY

I won't speak on my birth just know that with my presence
    I've blessed this earth
One of six kids, misunderstood
    survived it all and made it good in the hood
My moms frowned on me so early on
    it was hard for me to see I was different
    but my soul was still meant to be
I was told at a young age I would have it hard
    people mistreating me with no regard
    so I grew past those teenage years
    suffered through all my fears
Never knew the love of sister or brother
    because among them all I was the other
    child who stood alone and
    never called my house a home
These feelings I have are real
    sacred to me like gold to steel
I gave up trying to grab mom's attention
    the pressure was too much to mention
    so I left to go out on my own
    took care of myself like I was grown
    and damn, how can that be
    growing up fast, y'all, that was the key
I hit the books to elevate my mind
    knowing I would make them proud in time
    hoping I could change how they feel,
    and if it's all in vain, my heart it would kill
    this is who I am
I even gave part of my life to Uncle Sam
    years later I returned home to see
    if my journey had worked against me
All these year of tears
    I hope somebody hears me
    because grown now are we
    so let's stop all this rivalry

BAG LADY

I'm tired of carrying all these bags around.
I have them all, from very big to small.
I have a bag for laughter and a bag for tears.
I have a bag for all the good and bad years.
I have a bag full of pregnant stomachs and swollen ankles.
A bag for my marriage and the dreams it has mangled.
A bag for my many lovers and a big bag for the lies to cover.
There's a bag for my faults and a bag for my talents.
A bag for the career left in the balance.
I have a bag for that one true love I'm still looking for.
I will place him in it once he comes to my door.
I wish for a bag of tranquility because all this heaviness is getting the best of me. One day I will learn to travel light; without a care, there won't be a bag in sight.

WHAT I WANT

I want a man with eyes that can see the beauty beneath my skin and wrap himself in my spirit within

I want a man who can touch my sensuality; without using his hands, he'll have the best of me

I want a man who can hold my heart in his with just a simple kiss; at night when I'm alone, it's his lips I miss

I want a man who makes me feel I'm his all and all; for me he feels safe to fall

I want a man who just the thought of me makes his body quiver and his sexuality flows like a river

I want a man, y'all, who has the fear of God in his heart; of course spirituality is where it all starts

I want a man who has individuality, and making it with me is his only reality

I want a man with respect for me, no long nights out alone, by my side is where he should be

I want a man who can meet me on my level; hell, if he was in the Olympics, he would receive a gold medal

I want a man who knows struggle; he'll never fall by the wayside or bring me trouble

I want a man with just a touch of hood, to bring me loving that is so good

Yeah, I need a man like this, you see, because it would take a hell of a man to have a woman like me.

Yvonne Jackson (Allen)

A LETTER TO MY FATHER
(I Want to Come Home)

I've disappointed you so many times, fallen so far, I forgot what was mine, and each chance before that You've given me, I have cast it to the wind, killing every blessing from Thee. I won't last long out here in the wilderness; please help me, Lord, I need You to bless.

I want to come home, Lord, humbled in your way. I can't sleep at night any more; I'm lost in dismay. I want to come home, Jesus; with You I can see clearly. Your child sincerely.

Remembering the good times when I stood in Your good grace, fellowship and giving praises put a smile on my face. I think about those times to get me through. It was Your power, Lord, that I felt and knew. You held me in Your arms protected, and with Your grace and mercy, I was infected.

I want to come home, Lord, humbled in your way. I can't sleep at night any more; I'm lost in dismay. I want to come home, Jesus; with you I can see clearly. I am truly yours, Lord, sincerely.

Without you I will surely die;
> Stay in my life, don't pass me by. Take the blinders off so I can see. Build me up, set me free.

I want to come home, Lord; don't want to be lost any more. I'm empty inside and rotten to the core. I want to come home, Lord; with You, I am more than a conqueror. Don't want to leave here inferior.

I want to come home, Father, so I took this time to write You a letter. I need to come home and make this life better.

ABOUT THE AUTHOR

Yvonne Jackson, now Yvonne Allen, was born in Detroit, Michigan. She works for the federal government and is a proud U.S. Army veteran. Yvonne has been writing since she was a young girl. She has always had an appreciation for the arts in all forms.

A mother of five, Yvonne has what some people don't: a source to draw her stories from. Her two main categories of writing are fiction and poetry. Yvonne has written various articles and legal documents. She studied Media Arts Journalism at Long Island University in Brooklyn, N.Y.

A Circle of Sistaz: The Evolution of a Poet is the first installment of three volumes of poetry. Yvonne has much more to offer her readers, so keep your eyes open for future projects from this writer.

www.ingramcontent.com/pod-product-compliance
Lightning Source LLC
Chambersburg PA
CBHW070751050426
42449CB00010B/2416